Poetry Is a Painting in Words

Poetry Is a Painting in Words
A Collection of Poetry and Remembrances

BY Marjorie Nelson Sanford

COMPILED AND EDITED BY
Donna Blair Patterson

RESOURCE *Publications* · Eugene, Oregon

POETRY IS A PAINTING IN WORDS
A Collection of Poetry and Remembrances

Copyright © 2024 Donna Blair Patterson. All rights reserved. Except for brief quotations in critical publications or reviews, no part of this book may be reproduced in any manner without prior written permission from the publisher. Write: Permissions, Wipf and Stock Publishers, 199 W. 8th Ave., Suite 3, Eugene, OR 97401.

Resource Publications
An Imprint of Wipf and Stock Publishers
199 W. 8th Ave., Suite 3
Eugene, OR 97401

www.wipfandstock.com

PAPERBACK ISBN: 979-8-3852-3331-1
HARDCOVER ISBN: 979-8-3852-3332-8
EBOOK ISBN: 979-8-3852-3333-5

VERSION NUMBER 10/30/24

Preface

Marjorie Nelson Sanford was born on April 19, 1899, in the little village of Carlton, Pennsylvania, the last child born to James and Caroline Nelson. Throughout our family she was affectionately known as Aunt Margie. She spent her formative years in Franklin, Pennsylvania, under the guiding influence of her oldest sister and my grandmother, Nora. After high school graduation in 1918, Aunt Margie went to work for the New York Railroad where she spent fourteen years as a cashier. There she met Roy "Sandy" Sanford. They married in 1933. After Uncle Sandy's retirement, they bought a home in Cochranton, Pennsylvania.

During her marriage, Aunt Margie was a full-time housewife. Although she never had children of her own, she and Uncle Sandy always had dogs, upon whom they lavished as much attention as they would have any child. Every visit to their home included cocoa and cookies for all, and the dogs always got their share.

Uncle Sandy passed away in 1977. Two years later their last dog, Button, died of old age. Aunt Margie then decided to sell the house and move to an apartment in Corry, Pennsylvania, where she would be near family. It was a beautiful apartment across from the city park. She spent many days sitting in that park, thinking, reading and writing.

In 1986, Aunt Margie decided to move from the apartment into an assisted living home. I helped her dispense with her furniture and possessions, many of which went to other family members. But that last day she gave me a large notebook. It was filled with poetry and stories that she had written from the 1940's through 1984. Many of the poems had been published over the years in newspapers and magazines. In the years to follow, she would occasionally find another poem she had written and put away somewhere. It would be there when I went to visit. I'd then take it with me to add to her notebook.

On March 7, 1995, at the age of 96, Aunt Margie passed away, as quietly as she had lived. In preparation for her funeral, I read through her notebook. It was then that I began to really know her. Reading the words, I could hear her soft voice again, quietly comforting, wisely reassuring. Since that time, I have often pulled that notebook off the shelf, reaching for some wisdom or comfort to help me through a day. Now, Aunt Margie's words are here for you.

Requiem

Heaven must be crowded these days
With eager young souls newly arrived.
They look with wonderous amaze
On the vast spread of Paradise.
They pause hesitant, loathe to leave
The rumbling earth down below.
Yet, caught up in this celestial peace
Come to rest in God's glow.

1945

Aunt Margie wrote this when she was told that her nephew had been killed in World War II.

A Christmas Present

Four sisters have I and every one a jewel,
Each in her own special way.
First there is one who is wise in her counsel
And ready with helpful advice.
Next is a gal who can twist up a hat in nothing flat,
And give it to you with a smile.
Then there is one who is full of fun,
Enlivens every gathering.
Finally, she who wears her faith with lovely grace,
Steadfast and not faltering.
I have mentioned no names, so you pick out your verse.
In fact, they could apply to you all.
P.S. I could not extol my sisters without mentioning a brother
Who is quite a mister.
Tolerant, fair, and this above all rounds out the circle
Of a guy and four dolls.
Merry Christmas to all and to all a goodnight.

1950

Epitaph

I have gone into the far country, into the misty blue mountains.
The hot sands are shaken from my feet.
And now I'm in the leafy shade.
There is silence all about me.
The silence of centuries, and I am at peace.

1952

Chapeau Fleur

There's a hatful of roses atop my arbor
Perched there so saucily.
Green streamers of leaves fly in the breeze,
A la Schiaparelli!

1953

Spendthrift

The falling leaves like golden coins are flung across the lawn.
Prodigal season with gay abandon spends till all is gone.
Stripping the trees of all their glory
Till they stand naked and bare.
Do they know that spring will bring
Riches beyond compare?

1954

Lodestar

Tonight it is a golden moon.
A bright silver of gilt.
Creation's alloy with a heavenly sheen
Spun from celestial silt.
Tomorrow's orbit a silver bow,
Remotely pale, translucent.
But tonight a bright audacious star
Tells lovers to grasp this moment.

1954

Return

I walked to the edge of life today
And looked in the mists beyond.
Vague shadowy forms were passing there
Moving endlessly on and on.
I thought to join the shrouded throng
And take leave of all things mortal,
But they beckoned me not to walk with them,
And so, I closed death's portal.
And so, I closed death's portal.

1954

Korea

Send not the marks of death to me,
The cards, the flowers, the sympathy.
Let me keep this son alive in the heart of me.
The sun is still on his hair.
His smile will always be there.
Oh, dear ones, let me be.
Send not the marks of death to me.

1954

Autumn Leaves

A tapestry covers the hillside,
Red and yellow and tawny blending,
Creation's needlework tucked and folded
Over the hills never ending.
Each tree a stitch of color
Worked in with the Artist's skill.
A mantle of surpassing beauty
Thrown over rock and hill.
Season by season this miracle
Unfolds in wondrous glory,
Nature's fabric, divine handiwork
Tells the eternal story.

1956

Chapeaux

Milady Earth has many chapeaux, one for every occasion.
When she is gay, an azure cap with cloud-frond decoration.
For somber days a dove-gray affair sits soberly on her head
Ring'd with pendant raindrops and lined with sunset red.
But the prize of all is her evening bonnet,
A froth of cobalt blue.
All a'glitter with sequin stars
And pinned with a crescent moon.   1959

April Snow

April snow swirling down from the sky
Flock-dotting the landscape, winter's last goodbye.
A quick garnish for spring flowers gone in but an hour.
Hail and farewell. This is winter's dower.
1960

Love is . . . .

Love is a snare and delusion, a biological trap.
And anyone who falls for it is a dunderhead sap.
Love is a many splendored thing,
A lone idyllic dream,
A heavenly state of existence,
All stardust and moonbeams.
Love is wiping a wee little nose,
Whilst a cheery smile for the spouse,
When there is havoc and turmoil
All about the house.

1960

Limbo

I am so weary. Spare me heaven for awhile.
When death walks with me, let my head rest
On the deep pillow of oblivion.
Not for all eternity, just for an eon or two,
When the full glory of paradise will come to a rested soul.

1961

Immolation or Neutron Bomb

The deserted meadow with one barren tree,
Wears a lonely visage, patina of centuries.
No castle in the meadow.
No bird in the tree.
Only a vast emptiness
From the hills to the sea.
Just a brooding silence reaching for eternity,
A foretaste of the holocaust,
That is threatening humanity.

1961

Finale

Suddenly we realize that this is it, this and nothing more.
We braid up the remaining shred of life,
Tattered and torn as they are.
Lost ideals forsaken dreams, just a mirage of the mind.
This then, for the most part, is the lot of mankind.

1961

Cosmetics

Spring flounces in with her make-up kit
To renew winter's tired face.
She lightly dusts with a powder puff cloud
Promising all lines to erase.
A garland of violets she flings with abandon,
Pins a sunbeam in the hair.
Then the fickle creature sends the rains
And reduces all to despair.

1963

John F. Kennedy

So lately here the essence of his being surrounds us.
His voice lost in eternal silence
Whispers down the stairways
And speaks to us of peace.

1963

Robert F. Kennedy

Brother wait for me.
Let us walk together in this quiet place
And talk of other and happier times
Of brotherhood and of peace.

1968

Miniatures

The time tree casts it's elfin shadow
Across the lawn, the brave posturing of a child.
The minute shell rolls in with the tide,
A drop of the ocean against its heart.
The wee Babe waves his starfish hand
In a gentle arc and commands the universe.

1964

Aunt Net

She was very old.
She had passed the century mark.
In death, the casket enfolded her.
The shirred satin surrounds her frail body with gentleness.
There was dignity and grace in the folded hands,
Parchment thin.

1964

Circus

The sky, like a tent, is pegged down at the horizon.
A canvas for the circus we call life.
The clowns, the knaves, the saints and sinners
March around the tanbark in endless procession
And then make their exit.

1964

Non-Participant

She walks life's highway carefully, skirts the precipice cautiously,
views the scene dispassionately.
She stands aloof, an empty chalice, signifying nothing.

1967

Frippery

The jet streaks across the sky
Leaving miles of delicate lace in its wake,
A trimming for the robe of Heaven.

1967

Treasure

Like pressed flowers I lay away
My loved ones, one by one,
Between the pages of Heaven.

1967

Illusion

I awaken, standing knee-deep in dreams,
Separating fantasy from reality,
And wishing it were not so.

1967

Fortitude

I salute the whole human race.
They, for the most part,
Accept life with good grace.

1967

Look Forward Angel

I walk down the long corridor of time,
High vaulted rooms on either side
Filled with the debris of living,
And softly close each door.

1967

Flight

Birds soar to a pinnacle of flight
Then fall in a graceful arc,
Wheeling and turning in instant formation
Black confetti against the sky.

1967

Dissolution

A part of me breaks away
When a loved one dies.
I watch the bits and pieces disintegrate into memory,
Only then do I return to the living.

1967

Atom Bomb

Man grabs a handful of creation
And throws it Heavenward,
A puny probing of the infinite Universe.

1967

Minimum

I cast a tormented soul Heavenward,
Breaking into a million pieces against the stars,
Hoping a tiny fragment will find peace in the vast Universe.

1967

Epitome

I am content with this moment.
To look back is disaster, the future unknown.
This pinpoint of existence, dear God, let it suffice!

1967

Silence

The stillness of the day falls about me like a shroud,
And I am caught in its silken folds,
A whisper of eternity.

1967

Old Age

And now...
To the tag-ends of life,
The tarnished years edged with grief,
Interlaced with contentment.
A nice balance of joy and sorrow.
These are the later years.

1967

Silhouettes

The winter trees, like delicate black lace,
Edge the horizon silhouetted against the sky.
A light touch of fragile tracery in the bleak and frozen scene.

1968

Transition

The wagon wheels rumble to a full stop,
And I step down and sit by the side of the road and wait.
Presently ... a phantom carriage will approach silently,
And carry me away over the last horizon into eternity.

1968

Identity

The black man rages through the streets,
Looting, killing, burning,
His tattered soul a distillation of hatred garnered through the centuries.
The fires leap up to the sky,
Lighting up the face of Christ in a churchyard.
He smiles.
The face has been painted a beautiful black.
Let me climb into the skin of the black man.
Let me look out of this dusky façade,
At the prejudice of his brothers
And understand.

1968

Martin Luther King, Jr.

The bright rapier of the martyr
Slashed the moldering curtain of bigotry, prejudice and hatred
That hung dark and fouled for centuries,
Opening the way for the black man's march to freedom.

1968

Puzzlement

When I was young, I was told I'd be quite handsome as I grew old.
Now that I am old, I am informed, forsooth,
I must have been pretty in my youth!
So now I view my physiognomy with considerable perplexity.

1968

Christmastide

Dear little child of Bethlehem, touch us with thy tiny hand,
Thy gift a cradle of love this blessed Christmastide.

1968

Morning

The fog-enshrouded hills of a June morning,
A corrupt painting without a frame.

1968

Insomnia

The mind is a kaleidoscope.
Revolving facets of thought whirl through the brain,
Bending and interbending in bewildering sequence until sleep comes.

1968

Autumn

The autumn trees gaily appareled
Stand out against the storm- tossed winter sky
Like Christmas candles.

1969

Aging

We move along into old age,
Laying away our dead suitably adorned with flowers,
Tears of memory spilling,
The housekeeping of life and death.

1969

A Prayer

Lord, take my hand.
Walk with me for awhile.
I'll know of thy boundless love
And learn again how to smile.
No word is spoken.
None needs to be.
Father, take my hand.
Walk for awhile with me.

1969

In Passing

Our days fall like autumn leaves,
Some colorful, others drab,
Layer upon layer sinking into memory,
Enriching the mind as the lead-mold nourishes the earth.

1969

Respite

A rainy day wraps me in a soft embrace.
The mist-shrouded hills enfold me in their gentle arms,
And the world stands still . . . just for a minute.

1969

Haven

I like the snow. It is my refuge.
Nothing is expected when the blizzard whirls about me,
A soft cocoon into which I creep and go to sleep.

1969

Orbit

The moon voyagers spinning off into space,
Balanced on the rim of time,
Leave an agate marble suspended . . . the verdant earth.

1969

Happiness Is . . .

A will-of-the-wisp
Darting in and out of the fabric of living
Like quicksilver.

1969

Fabric

Gather together all the loose ends of life
And weave them into a whole.
Form and substance will take place
And give surety to the soul.

1969

Indecision

Death is walking with us today.
He may stay, and he may go away.
He stands on the slim edge of time,
A delicate balance in this celestial clime.

1969

Verity

The magic of growing things,
The subtle shadings, the blossomings,
Who figured it all out?
The pale blue silk of the sky,
Assorted clouds roll by,
Who figured it all out?
The verdant green of a stately tree,
What color could it be?
Who figured it all out?
This divine spark that is within me,
That lifts my soul to infinity,
Who figured it all out?
Who can deny God?

1969

Why?

The spin-off into space
Leaves the mottled earth in its wake,
Revolving in its own blood,
To explore a dry husk,
Planet moon . . . a geologist's paradise.

1969

I Wonder

Am I dying well?
Am I joining my two worlds together with neat precision,
The known and the unknown,
One smooth and swift transition,
Done with courage and grace
Worthy of thee.

1969

Imperfection

There is a perfection in imperfection,
End of day bric-a-brac fashioned from leftover scraps of glass,
Each individual and lovely in its own right.
An impressionistic painting,
A mere blob on close view,
Yet, seen at a distance, a thing of beauty.
A few words strung together
Loosely called a poem,
May bring comfort to a troubled mind.
A flawed soul,
Prostrate at the foot of the Cross,
Receives forgiveness and is made whole again.

1969

Reincarnation

When flowers die,
I lay them gently on the ground.
There to return to the soil that gave them birth.
Tiny candles of Heaven to light the way to endless beauty.

1969

The Wind

Blow wind blow, exultant and wild,
Heart of the storm, hurricane's child.
Scudding the clouds
Above the tall trees,
Shifting the scene
Along the airways.
High-riding and free,
I envy you so,
As I watch
From here below.
Blow wind, blow,
Soft and mild,
Dies to a whisper
And is reconciled.

1969

U.S.A . . . .This Wondrous Land

This land, this wondrous land,
Which dabbles its fingers in the Atlantic and Pacific,
Wears a crown of Alaskan snow,
And warms its feet in the Gulf of Mexico.
The majestic mountains dipping into peaceful valleys
And the plains swept clean with the winds of Heaven.
The shimmering lakes set like precious jewels in this golden land.
The trees holding the land in their firm grip,
Redwoods that the baby Jesus could have touched with his tiny hand.
The tapestry of fall colors
Laid so carefully over the hills,
Beauty that wishes the soul clean.
Oh! This land . . . this wondrous, glorious land.

1970

Charisma

We are stripped to the bare bones in old age.
The artful paddings of vanity and conceit fall away.
We stand forth in all truth as a child again.

1970

The Rebels

The young rebels spewing their obscenities,
Scrounging in filth,
Tearing bodies limb from limb with their bombs.
The pseudo-intellectuals would lead us back to the primitive cave,
Fighting for the last morsel of flesh from the latest kill,
While gazing out in a world devastated.

1970

Withdrawal

I gather together the four corners of my world,
And tie them in a tidy bow,
Encased in a mindless void . . . lest the heart break.

1970

Words

Words are written on the walls of the mind
That can only be erased by God.

1970

Necklace

I push the days by like beads on a string,
Some base metal, others pure gold,
And lay it on the altar of eternity.

1970

Eventide

The sun reaches out long pink fingers,
Gathering in the horizon in a blaze of glory,
Never the same again.
In the realm of time,
Changing from rose to mauve to gray,
Until the sable curtain of night descends.

1970

Reckoning

A time for laughter and a time for sorrow,
One follows the other tomorrow and tomorrow.
A time for folly and a time for reason,
One follows the other season upon season.
A time for living and a time for dying,
One follows the other till the final reckoning.

1971

Airborne

Skim over the lake of despair,
Fly up through the clouds of hope,
Ascend to blue tranquility,
Level off on the Elysian slopes.

1971

The Pond

The pond, like a silver button,
Lost in the deep forest,
Reflects the changing moods of the sky.
I stir its murky depths
And wish it were not so,
It did not merit defilement.

1971

Sanctuary

I have come to this island,
For the rest of my life,
I will forget all about it,
This world's storm and strife.
I've raged up and down
The streets of the world,
Now I've laid down my trophies,
My banners are furled.
Quiet waters lap at the shore,
As I watch the scene passing by.
I will stay on my island,
Forever more until I die.

1971

The Lake

Dancing diamonds on the water,
Ring'd with emerald green,
A scintillating jewel fit for a queen.

1972

Sorrow

Sorrow bites deeply,
Recedes and returns,
Each time diminishing
Until it is bearable.

1972

The Day

The day creeps on,
Like the wave of the ocean,
Greedily eating up
The sands of time.

1972

Ghost Dogs

Careening down the garden path to greet me,
What a glorious reunion,
Patsy, Cindy, Briar, Sandy Boy, Mike and Button I and II,
Years of boundless devotion,
Living memories caught in a prism of time.

1973

Verities

The miracle of growing things,
The subtle blendings, the flowerings,
Who figured it all out?
The pale blue silk of the sky
With assorted clouds floating by,
Who figured it all out?
The verdant green of a stately tree,
What other color could it be?
Who figured it all out?
Who can deny God?

1973

Sanctuary

I reach up and gather the blue folds of Heaven about my ears.
I reach out and make a mantle of the trees of the forest.
I kneel down and rest on the comforting earth.
This is my shield and fortress.

1973

Emissary

At times I feel quite sure,
There's a wee guardian angel perched on my shoulder.
He smiles at my whims and frowns at my foibles,
But he's in there pitching when I am really in trouble.
Some may feel this is a light approach
To the almighty power of God,
But I like to think his emissaries
Are always on the job.

1973

Crescendo

I wash a dish and make a bed,
Look at the stars and wish I were dead.
So, I plant a flower and wrap a gift,
Feed the birds, my spirits lift.
I give to the poor and help a friend,
Say a kind word, I'm on top again.

1973

Frustration

The most powerful thought comes to me for a divine bit of poetry.
I soar aloft with the muses and rapture my soul suffuses.
But when I try to make the thing rhyme,
I cannot get beyond the first line!

1973

Surrender

Sometimes...
I feel like crumpling up my life like a piece of scrap paper
And throwing it as far as I can.
But I know I will have to pick it up,
Spread it out, and start living again.

1974

Respite

This is a day that has no yesterdays or tomorrows.
It is caught eternally in a prism of time,
A soul's respite, an oasis of the mind.

1974

Shut-In

I did not see all the fall colors,
Only one timely sampling,
But, oh the glory of that scarlet tree,
From my window's viewing.
The epitome of all the glorious beauty
That covers the hills.

1974

God

The ever-inscrutable Deity, who gives us the limitless sky,
That stretches to the edge of the universe.
But how can there be an end to something that is endless?
This mystery is the beginning and the ending,
From the first stirrings of life eons ago,
To the ultimate soul and to life eternal.

1974

The Journey

Whither goest thou, little girl with the dancing feet,
Rope skipping down the busy street?
Whither goest thou, lass of sixteen,
Full of high hopes and a pocketful of dreams.
Whither goest thou,
Lady of great age,
Living with your memories turning the last page.
Whither... goest... thou?

1974

Morning Magic

The silver frost lays a sparkling wall-to-wall carpet
Over the frozen grass,
Makes shining buttons of tiny puddles,
And touches the countryside with a soft hand.
All the roughness of the earth is now gently defined,
And everywhere is magic.

1974

Humanity

Lumps of clay dredged up from the primal ooze,
Fashioned in different shapes and sizes,
And imbued with a divine spirit.
We don't always understand
Struggling, hating, loving,
And sometimes touched with a miracle.
Lumps of clay dissolving into dust,
But the soul marches on.

1975

Symphony

The music flows like living waters,
Swirling into the hollows of the mind.
The flute notes as a dancing brook,
Through the senses gently wind.
Then the ever-widening river of sound
Leaps to the crescendo of the mighty sea,
And the soul is lifted up in a wave of ecstasy.

1975

Redemption

The golden cross gleams in the sterile sanctuary,
Chaste, pure, untouched.
We sit in formal rows attending to the ritual.
Suddenly I am on Calvary,
I see through timbers lashed together,
With a torn and broken figure suspended, crucified,
The ultimate torture.
My tears mingle with his,
And the soul is eternally cleansed.

1975

Containment

Around and around the time clock goes,
Summer winds and winter snows,
Fickle spring and autumn sublime.
Quarter seasons neatly defined.
Would that our lives could be ordered so,
Then no heartbreak overflow.

1975

Memories

We fill the bottle of life with glee,
Gay abandon and ecstasy,
Brimming with gusto, laughter and tears,
Collectibles garnered through the years.
Then we pour it all out one day
And watch it slowly trickle away.

1975

Life Span

We dump all our experiences
Into the great vat of time.
Life gives it a stir,
And we live with our memories.

1976

Remembrance

The weight of the years
Packs us down solidly
Into a box
Of remembrance.

1976

Promises

The sky is dismal and gray, but the promise is there,
Azure blue and sunset red, and dazzling rainbow so fair.
The trees are stripped of their splendor, but the promise is there,
Tiny, budding green leaves, and autumn colors beyond compare.
The seed lies fallow on the ground, but the promise is there,
Fragrant flowers of every hue, scenting the summer air.
The cross stood on a desolate hill, but the promise was there,
Forgiveness for a contrite soul, and God's love everywhere.

1976

Solution

With all this flap about the whites and the blacks,
The thought occurred to me one day.
Why can't we forget the color syndrome
And all be considered just gray.

1977

Salvage

I reach out for bits and pieces of happiness
Amidst the stress of living
And hoard them carefully
Against the time of memory.

1977

The Bond

Sorrow is a great leveler.
It brings us all into the same camp.
King or common, we join hands
And bow our heads in grief,
 Together.

1977

Polish

We start out with a great chunk of life,
 Spending it freely
With no thought of tomorrow.
A love here, a folly there,
Chipping away until we come to the end
With a small, smooth pebble of memories.

1979

Random Thought

Making something out of nothing.
Always leave a place better than you find it.
Perfectionists are a pain in the neck.
It isn't what happens to you that counts,
 It is how you take it.
 Work against the odds.

1979

Adversaries (First Version)

Life skips merrily down the garden path,
Unafraid of a distant shrouded figure,
Death.
In time she turns and meets him eye to eye.
There is no fear, nor even any dismay.
Death is not the conqueror.
It is only a passing phase,
Until that glorious day
When we see the Savior's face.

1981

The Journey (Adversaries—Second Version)

Life skips merrily down the garden path,
Unaware of a distant figure,
Death.
He draws closer as time goes by.
Life turns fearfully.
It is too soon to die.
But time won't wait and the specter comes closer.
Life and death clasp hands,
And the journey is over.

1981

Rock-a-bye Baby ... the M.S. Version

Rock-a-bye baby off to dream land.
Eyes gently closing. Comes the sandman.
Rock-a-bye baby held in my arms,
Cozy and warm.
Safe in my arms.

1982

Author's note: Dumping a baby out of a treetop doesn't seem very conducive to sleep. Hence the new version.

Time

Fleeting time, I feel like grabbing chunks of it,
And stowing them away like a squirrel for future use.
It goes so fast, and I am caught in a maelstrom
Of flying seconds, minutes, hours, until there is nothing left.
And I have run out of time.
Layers and layers of living,
Pressed down and overflowing
Into a potpourri of memory.

1982

While Soaking in the Tub

Let my mind float free of life's anxieties.
Let my mind wander in Elysian fields
Until my sore spirit heals.
But then I must return with a thud... and scrub!

1983

A Tribute to Jessica Savitch

Jessica, with the smiling eyes,
Forging a bond with her audience,
Instant empathy.
She closed her newscast with a cheery goodnight,
And so, I say for one last time,
"Goodnight, Jessica."

1983

Today

Today has two doors, yesterday and tomorrow.
Lock the door on yesterday.
Don't open tomorrow.
Contend with today.
Life in small portions is bearable.

1984

Chapters

I have closed many chapters in my life,
But God, in His own good time,
Will close the book.

1984

Geriatric Jitters

Names, events, dance on the fringe of my memory.
They elude me, and I am frustrated.
Is this what they call senility?
Yesterday floats into the subconscious.
I search for remembrance and am lost.
Is this an exercise in futility?
Perhaps the pigeon holes of the mind are full to capacity,
And we must contend with satiety.

1984

The Quiet Path

They break away from the teaming masses,
Some bewildered, others defiant.
Those who are resigned and the myriad of souls who are at peace.
They are alone for a brief moment.
Then a companion joins them.
Soon others will appear,
And they walk together into eternity.
This constant wave of humanity like a field of wheat,
Is laid low for the Harvester,
And a new generation springs forth to walk the same well-worn path.

1984

Autumn

October was a spend-thrift and giddier than most.
She spilled her bounty everywhere then vanished,
Now her ghost, November, born and frugal, is briefly all that's left.
One solitary leaf against a branch....bereft.

1984

Famous "Aunt Margiesms":
Poetry is a painting in words.
Nature spills the perfume bottle in June.

Aunt Margie's favorite quotation:
2nd. Timothy, Chapter 4, Verse 7: "I have fought the good fight.
I have finished my course. I have kept the faith."

I Remember Grandma

It has been said that we should not visit the scenes of our early childhood in later years as we usually are in for a disappointment. We all, I think, have a habit of cloaking the early scene in a lovely haze, glossing over everything but the pleasant and beautiful.

But I can't say I was affected this way when, one day, not so long ago, I rode up the long lane to the site of my maternal grandmother's home. The house had long since gone by fire and only the foundation remained. The rough stones were grown over with grass and wildflowers, a remnant of a picket fence lay partially hidden in the tangle of the weeds, but the outline of the garden was still there. As I stood and looked down into what was once the cellar, a host of memories came back to me.

The house had been what is called a salt-box type of a nondescript color aged through the years until it blended with the landscape and was part of it. We always used the kitchen entrance as it was unthinkable to go in the front way. That was reserved for weddings and funerals and such auspicious occasions.

The kitchen wasn't too large. My mind's eye placed the large, shining wood stove in a dim corner, a table under the window, and the clock overhead on the shelf. I can still remember the particular sound of that clock as it sounded off the hours. It struck high and quick as if it were anxious to get the task done with. It sort of fitted in with grandmother's character, which was energetic, with a bit of impatience mixed in.

Grandmother was small with the tiniest feet imaginable, but there was a lot of force packed in that small frame. Her house and garden were immaculate, dust nor weed never being countenanced under her stern vigilance. She was a little self-opinionated, having strong views on certain subjects, particularly the interpretation of the Bible. She would argue with the deacons of the little church, which stood up the road a mile or so, and, I think, would have had the temerity to stand up to the Almighty, Himself.

I can remember, in later years, when she came to visit us, it was always my duty to accompany her to prayer meeting. I suppose I was about ten years old at the time. Those were the days of long testimonials in the church we attended. I can distinctly remember pulling at her skirt when I thought she had said enough. Even at my tender age, I recognized the slightly concerned expression on the preacher's face as the service lengthened out. I cannot readily understand why my mother sent me with grandmother. Mother's religion was of a more placid, restful type, and, being very self-effacing, the testimonials must have been a little embarrassing to her.

Those weekly visits to prayer meetings also bring to mind the little lace caps grandmother use to wear in summer. Her hair was very thin, and she would wear it to protect her head. In order to hear better, she would push the cap up on one side which would give her a slightly rakish air. This also caused me some concern.

It comes to mind at this point, that, in our church, it used to be the custom for any member of the congregation to give out with a good, hearty "Amen" during the prayer service. I can't help but think what consternation would result if someone were to do that in our church today. The passing years have laid a decorous hand on us.

I like to recall the different rooms in grandmother's house. Off the kitchen there was a small bedroom. There stood the trundle bed and the high chest with the huge two drawers. The rest of the room fades off into the shadows like the kitchen. Memory seems to highlight certain things.

A large living room led off the kitchen, and here is where the family gathered. I don't remember too much about the furniture except a cupboard in the corner, which held the good dishes. They had a copper luster band and clover design in the center. To me they were quite elegant as I gazed at them through the glass. Off this room to the left, was the holy of holies, the parlor. The what-not in the corner with its seashells, tea cups and the like, the small Victorian sofa, the Brussels carpet on the floor, all were viewed from the doorway. Under no circumstances was I to enter. I did tiptoe in one day and lifted one of the tiny cups, but my heart was pounding for fear of discovery. Grandmother was not very kind to me, but I knew she meant what she said.

To the rear of the parlor was what was called the parlor bedroom. This, too, was carpeted and a huge comfortable bed stood across the corner. My dearest impression of this room was a handsome chamber pot with lovely pink roses on its side, sitting just under the bed.

The attic was a place redolent with the smell of cured hams and bacon hanging from the rafters. When the house overflowed with company, the children were put there to sleep. It was rather an eerie sensation to wake in the night and see those ghostly shapes hanging above your head.

All around the house stood a picket fence. Within its confines were lovely flowers of every variety. To one side was a vegetable garden with the beds built up by Grandma's careful hands. I can still see her patting and rounding up the paths and removing every weed before it had a chance.

Out beyond this garden, there was a meadow where I use to love to wander. I can close my eyes now and see the timothy and daisy heads waving above me as I laid on my back looking up at the blue sky, thinking long, long thoughts of youth. Tiring of that, I would wander down the road to a little plank bridge. Underneath was the coolest spot imaginable. You could watch by the hour the minnows in the clear, sparkling water. I even tried to catch one with a bent pin on a string, but I have no recollection of success.

Then there was always the dim, cool barn where Grandfather held sway. He was a soft-spoken, kindly man with the traditional long gray beard. The one horse and cow were cared for gently and efficiently. What a peaceful existence for a little girl to absorb.

On the way back from the barn, there was the customary two-holer, scrubbed bone white. I don't remember any Sears Roebuck catalog, but there were neat squares of paper hanging on a hook.

A pig pen was in the offing somewhere, but I always made a wide detour around that. I have no doubt Grandma scrubbed them too, along with everything else, but they were still pigs to me.

After a long and glorious day of such wanderings, there was early supper. Sometimes delicious home cured ham or simply mush and milk, but nothing has tasted so good since. Then to bed to dream of another long peaceful day when, as Robert Browning has said:

> "The year's at the spring;
> And the day's at the morn;
> Morning's at seven;
> The hillside's dew pearled;
> The lark's on the wing;
> The snail's on the thorn;
> God's in His Heaven;
> All's right with the world."

Full Circle

Memory flashes back through time with the speed of light to incidents highlighted by some special importance. Such an occasion comes to mind which concerns my eldest sister, Eleanora, named for her Grandmother Nelson and soon shortened to Nora by the family. I was the youngest with four sisters and two brothers in between and two deceased brothers. The occasion was the event of her wedding.

    I, being all of five years old, was all agog with excitement. It was held in the evening in the parlor of our home. I remember the chairs being arranged in rows, and I must have been constantly underfoot as this was a totally new experience to me. I flew upstairs and into the bedroom where Nora, with the help of female relatives, was getting dressed for the nuptials. She was pulling on long white cotton stockings with a black embroidered design on them, then high-topped laced black shoes. About this time, I was discovered and summarily ousted. I have been told her wedding dress was cream silk which she had made, as well as all her trousseau, which was of very fine needlework. Strange to say, I remember nothing of the ceremony. Perhaps my little five-year old brain could take only so much. And so, Eleanora Nelson and Homer Blair were united in marriage.

    He had rented a house at the corner of Eighth and Buffalo Streets, a rather large one, and they in turn rented the upstairs rooms. There was a small barn in the back yard where Homer kept a horse and buggy. He was a graduate of Grove City College, had taught school briefly, and was studying law in the office of Donald B. McCalmont. His parents, Mary and George Blair, lived in Clintonville where he had been raised. There is an amusing incident about the horse. There being no inside toilet in the house, Nora would set out the various receptacles in the morning for airing. One day, the horse planted his foot firmly in one of the pots demolishing it!

Their first child, Donald Burnett, named for Homer's benefactor, was born in this house, and events pertaining to that birth caused a break in family relations that lasted for several years. My widowed mother, who by this time, was working as a maternity nurse, was taking care of Nora. Homer objected very strongly to some of the methods of caring for a woman after child birth and asked her to leave. I can remember being routed out of bed (she, of necessity, had taken me with her) and walking home in the darkness, tightly clasping her hand. Mary Blair was, no doubt, to blame for Homer's archaic notions about childbirth. She was a rather narrow-minded, bigoted woman whose god was money. Since we were "poor as church mice", we stood pretty low on the totem pole in her estimation. My mother very quietly withdrew from the situation without any recrimination, and carefully avoided being in Nora's home when Homer as there.

In due course of time, a second son was born who lived only twenty-four hours. He was a "blue baby" and could have been saved with the knowledge the medical profession has nowadays. He was not named which I thought was a pity as he should have had an identity.

A short time later, Homer bought a house on Eighth Street near the Allegheny River. The house was fairly old, "salt box" in design with a sloping roof on the back. He loved gardening and really had a large, outstanding one. I remember he raised celery, which was unusual then, and even had peanuts one year. This was his hobby, and he would go straight through the house in the evening, leaving a trail of coat, tie, and shirt, on the way to uproot any weeds that may have appeared. The neighbors also had gardens, and they would vie with each other to have the first ripe tomato. In the evening they would gather in the ally at the rear of the property to play horseshoes. I can still hear the ring of the shoe as it hit the peg. It was a truly peaceful existence.

Nora's proclivity for interior decorating began to be apparent in those early days. The living room was furnished with Mission style furniture (now being sold as antiques) with two walls lined with book shelves. Homer collected books other than legal tomes. The walls were a soft yellow and was an easy and comfortable room to relax in. In those days, one must have a parlor to entertain callers. Nora, through careful juggling of household money, had acquired an upright piano, a round mahogany table and rocker. The floor was covered with a very pretty rose-colored Brussels rug. It needed more, of course, and the ingenious mind of the lady of the house got herself some lumber and hewed out two very acceptable easy chairs. After she built the frames, she covered them with a rose design tapestry. This encouraged her to build a desk for the living room which was of a most unique design. Homer was of no help to her as he had no aptitude for carpentry. I don't know what became of those pieces of furniture. They just disappeared into the mists of time.

Don was a quiet, introspective boy who loved the things of nature. He would climb the hill at the end of Eighth Street bridge and bring home wild flowers for his garden. One time he brought back a bull frog to put in a pool in the center of his garden. It gallumped all night, causing some insomnia in the neighborhood. Fortunately, it was gone by morning. He started to school, which was then on the corner of Ninth and Elk Streets. All seemed well until a neighbor told Nora that Don was going down to the river and staying until it was time to go home. His parents took him to task, and he said he was afraid of his teacher, Miss McDonald. I had gone to her, and she was a real tyrant. I can still see her coming down the aisle with a three-cornered ruler to crack someone over the knuckles. She was truly a sadist. The problem with Don was resolved, and when he went to the next grade, he settled into school work with pleasure and was always a good student.

But after a few years, tragedy struck. Homer became ill with Bright's disease, an ailment of the kidneys, for which there was no cure at that time. During his illness, he bought an automobile, and Oldsmobile I believe. Nora learned to drive so she could take him for country rides which he dearly loved. I think Nora was one of the first, if not the first, woman to drive a gasoline powered car in Franklin. A few women, at that time, were zipping around town in small, elegant cars with a handle bar to guide them, and usually a bud vase with a rose in it hung inside.

Homer's illness finally took its toll, and he died on a cold winter's day in 1916 at the age of thirty-seven. Shortly before his death, he suggested to Nora that mother and I come to live with her after he was gone. This was his gesture of friendship toward mother because, by this time, he recognized her innate goodness. He was always very kind to me, and I spent many happy hours in their home. I was just six years older than Don, so we were more like brother and sister.

After Homer's death, Nora was a very sad and broken young woman. It took some time to come back to the living. My mother, brother Joe, and myself did move in with Nora for a year or so, then we moved to an apartment nearby. She was busy with closing Homer's office and determining what her assets would be. The estate was not too large, but there was income from oil leases near Clintonville and half interest in the Park Theater. Homer had entered into partnership with Tom Kinney some years before his death.

After a time, Nora's fertile brain was planning the remodeling of her house, and she really made an exquisite home. She literally raised the roof of the house, converting it into a Dutch Colonial, allowing for four nice bedrooms. The partition between the living and the dining rooms was removed making a very spacious living room. The former parlor became the dining room. The breakfast nook was quite an innovation in those days, so she designed the kitchen to accommodate one. The living room was really outstanding. The walls were paneled in white with a red brick fireplace on the outer wall. French doors were at either end and rose velvet drapes were hung at the windows. Tapestries were paneled into the walls at three different locations which added a very distinctive note. I believe Homer had brought the tapestries home from a business trip. Nora's talent for producing beautiful interiors was burgeoning into existence.

I was a proud possessor of a pass to the Park Theater. Those were the days of the "Perils of Pauline", a cliff-hanger serial, which I would agonize over week after week. Marie Dressler, Mary Pickford, Fatty Arbuckle, Douglas Fairbanks, and John Barrymore were just a few of the stars. The serials were in the afternoon, and I would fly to the theater after school. Then, Nora, Don, and I would go in the evening quite frequently and walk home together on cold winter nights, or in the beauty of a summer evening. Our mother never quite accepted the movies.

A few years went by uneventfully, until a house across the street from Nora on the corner of Eighth and Elk was for sale. It was considered one of the oldest houses in Franklin. I have just a dim memory of a rather plain, nondescript edifice, but Nora saw possibilities. So, it was purchased, and she transformed it into a very attractive, livable home. One interesting note about the place was the unusually large stones in the foundation. It was theorized but not proven that they could have come from the fort that was located on the site many years before. In due course of time, Nora sold her home and lived in the house just renovated for some time. There was a large lawn about the house, and Nora had purchased a privet hedge to enclose the whole property. She asked Don to plant it. It seemed he had planned a fishing trip but the hedge must be done. Nora had often remarked that she never saw anything planted so rapidly. Every plant grew and is still in existence!

Eventually, Nora and Mr. Kinney, the co-owner of the Park Theater, entered into an agreement to exchange her holding in the theater for his house located on Buffalo Street. It was a very large, well-built home near the business district. She immediately re-modeled it into three apartments, one of which the Kinney family occupied. Later Nora made it possible for mother and I to move into one of the apartments at a very nominal rent. It was a very happy time in mother's life as she was near town and her beloved City Park. I think I should interject an incident at this point. A celebration, Old Home Week, I believe, was to take place, and Mrs. Blair, Homer's mother, wanted to attend the festivities. It was arranged for her to stay with us as a grand parade would pass the house. We had two bedrooms but, since one was rented, mother and I would occupy the same room. It was large and comfortable with an extra bed, but Mary snored, and I really mean she raised the rafters! After a sleepless night, mother and I were desperate. But Nora came to the rescue with ear-muffs. It was bearable after that. There was a very good development from this encounter. Mary appreciated mother's hospitality, and there was a good relationship formed between them.

Shortly after Nora had acquired the Kinney house, a large Victorian mansion on Fifteenth Street was for sale. It had been built by Charles Miller, known as General Miller, and was probably constructed in the 1880's. He had made his fortune in oil and had made quite an impact on the economic and social scene in Franklin. Some years before, he had started a real estate development known as Miller Park and had built a large, magnificent home there which he was now occupying. Nora became interested in the Fifteenth Street property and, consequently, purchased it. She was soon involved in remodeling it into six apartments. The rooms were spacious with fireplaces in many of them. Beautiful parquet floors were laid in the main rooms. There were two apartments on the first floor, three on the second, and one on the third. All the original beauty of the home was kept intact. Nora made full use of her ability to transform the home into modern usage without destroying the Victorian charm. There was no difficulty in renting the apartments as they were in great demand. This was the "Roaring Twenties", and money flowed freely.

As a person who loved beautiful interiors, Nora had quite an interest in antique furniture, and consequently, she started to collect and sell on a large scale. She remarked one day that her philosophy of life was "to jump into the middle of a project and wade out".

Some of the furniture would be in bad condition, so she kept two workmen busy repairing and refinishing. Her antique shop was not a grubby, dusty affair, as so many of them were, but a well-run and lucrative business. The refinished pieces would be brought into her apartment and shown there amidst beautiful surroundings.

By this time, I was making my home with my sister, as our mother, after a three-month illness, had passed away in September, 1926. Her casket stood in one of the lovely rooms, which was a fitting surrounding for this wonderful lady.

Nora and I would start out in her little Essex coupe to scour the countryside for antique glass and china. She had heard of a Mr. Cozad near Mercer who had some things. So, we headed there one Saturday afternoon. I was employed at the New York Central Railroad during the week. True enough, he had some good pieces, one of which was a slant top desk with inlaid wood. She decided we could put it in the trunk of the car. Mr. Cozad, who must have been close to eighty years old, was tying it with a rope. As he pulled to secure it, the rope broke, and he went "head over tater top" (an old expression). We rushed to pick him up fearing he was hurt, and he brushed us off saying he wasn't hurt a bit. A very independent soul! When he got the desk lashed into place again, he invited us to stay for supper. His wife had to be away, but she had left things prepared. So, we sat down to stewed chicken and elderberry pie in the corner of the kitchen. I have that desk in my home today as a gift from my sister.

Those were the halcyon years. People were making fortunes on paper in the stock market. The bootleggers were thriving in the sale of illicit liquor because of prohibition laws. President Hoover was telling us that all was well with our country. People were dancing the Charleston, and we were rolling our stockings below our knees with short skirts yet! A gay, happy time which soon ended. In the fall of 1929, the stock market started to weaken, and soon it was an avalanche. Fortunes were lost in a few hours, and people committed suicide. The bubble had burst, and the good times were gone. Fortunately, this did not affect Nora as she owned no stocks. But tragedy struck from another source in 1930.

One summer evening a fire started in the walls of the apartment house, was soon out of control, and the building was a total loss. It had to be defective wiring, or a tenant had put a copper penny in his fuse box. He had been caught at this earlier and warned. We saved some furniture from the first floor, very little from the second, and none from the third floor. I remember standing quite near a large brick chimney on the side of the house for a moment and, as I started to leave, it fell in a sharp heap. It surly would have killed me if I had been a few seconds later. Luckily no one else was near it. It is all still very painful to recall. The walls of the house were left standing by the fire and were pulled down later.

Our Aunt Ella offered us shelter, and we stayed with her for several weeks. Nora was still in a state of shock, but, true to her nature, she kept her balance figuring out what to do. As it sometimes happens in life, a solution was at hand. French Miller, the son of General Miller, who was now deceased, approached her about leasing the General's home in the Park. It was now closed with caretakers in charge. She went to see the home and found an elegant residence in good condition. It was an English half-timber and brick construction on the outside. The floors were all carpeted with large oriental rugs in the hallway and an enormous oriental rug in the library. The drawing room and reception room were paneled with brocades, and the banquet hall was done in shades of lavender. We were told there was a dinner service and glassware especially designed for this room. The General had built and furnished this home when he was in his heyday. Later, financial reverses brought him down, and he died a pauper. All of his holdings had liens against them, including this home.

Nora toured the house, and her active mind began planning how it could be arranged, temporarily, to take care of her tenants. There were plenty of bathrooms and three kitchens. She contacted the tenants, and they all agreed to move in. After the horror of the fire, it was rather an adventure. French and Clarence Miller were so very helpful and, I think, happy to have the house occupied. They aided us in every possible way. After a year or so there was some remodeling to make it more convenient which was planned and supervised by Nora.

It became evident about this time that my sister's health was not good. She went to a doctor who, upon examination, found heart damage. The whole impact of the fire and the financial losses were taking its toll. She went into a nervous collapse which invalided her for several years. The Depression was in full swing now, and the spirit of the country and its people was at low ebb. I was laid off as cashier at the railroad office, so another income was lost. Don was struggling to establish a radio business. The tenants could not pay their rent, but somehow, we managed to get coal for the large furnace, and we ate regularly. Many people went hungry in those days.

As time went by, the economic situation improved somewhat. President Roosevelt got the country going again. I had married by this time and was living in Pittsburgh. Leota Hendershot, a cousin, came to stay with Nora as she was still quite frail.

Just back of the "big house" as we called it was a residence which had been built for the servants. It was also of brick and half-timber construction with ivy covered walls. We called it the "Cottage" to distinguish it from the large house, but it was quite spacious with six large rooms and one- and one-half baths. Nora, by this time, found the management of the large house tiring, so, when the cottage was empty, she arranged to rent it. The inside needed papering and painting and, as the rent was very reasonable, she became interested in redecorating it herself. It was a decided lift to her spirits to be creative again. In one end of her home would be her sitting room, bedroom and bath. Upstairs were two large bedrooms and a bathroom.

When it came time to move in, I came up from Pittsburgh to be of help. We got all the furniture, rugs and curtains in place, then brought her up to see the results. I shall never forget the expression on her face when she walked into her sitting room. She looked so happy and remarked, "Now I am home". The sun came in through the ruffled curtains and danced on the cheery yellow walls. Her cherished honey colored pine furniture was all in place. The big house had its grandeur, but it was never home.

Thus, she settled into a rather peaceful decade. Visits from family and friends kept her from being lonely. She kept herself occupied with light housekeeping chores (Leota had left to be married) and her needlework. This had been a special interest of hers since she was very young. Before she was married, she had taken a course in dressmaking in Cleveland and did sewing for the general public. She was also an expert in millinery. Now her talents turned to making quilts, hooked rugs, and crocheted articles. All of the family has many things from her nimble fingers, especially table mats of which she must have made dozens.

During this time her son, Don, and Helen Kiskadden were married, and, in 1939, a little red-headed baby girl was born named Judith Ann. Now Nora's life took on new meaning with this beloved grandchild. In time, she discussed with Don the possibility of having his own home for his family. He was loathed to leave her alone, but, by this time, she felt capable of managing by herself. So, some land was purchased outside of Franklin, and a house was built. Judy, along with her husband and three children, live in this house today. (Editor's note: As of 2022, Judy's son, Chris, now lives in this home which is referred to by the family as "the homestead".)

World War II was rumbling around the world, and we were all preoccupied with this terrible holocaust. A nephew, Charles Reed, was a casualty of this war, losing his life in Germany. He was awarded the Silver Star for exceptional bravery.

Finally, this insanity of Hitler and the Japanese war lords was over, and we all began trying to live normal lives again. Nora came to the decision to move downtown where she could attend church and the Women's Club and take more part in community activities. Consequently, she rented an apartment at Liberty and Eleventh Streets. It was on the second floor and was very comfortable, but she never really settled in. It wasn't just what she wanted.

There always seemed to be a pattern of circumstances in her life that brought the change that was needed. Don stopped in one day in 1945 and remarked, "Mother, how would you like to live again in the house where I was born?" He went on to say that it was not in very good condition. So, it was arranged to see the house, and Don's evaluation was certainly the understatement of the year. It was terribly rundown and incredibly filthy. But Nora, as usual, saw the possibilities and the purchase was made.

Don added kitchens for the two apartments and a bathroom downstairs, also a utility room. After cleaning the house thoroughly, it was painted and papered inside and out. Now it was ready for occupancy. Nora moved in, and, after a time, began to visualize some changes to make it more to her liking. Don would only take a small rental, so she proceeded at her own expense. She transformed the living room by adding a wide cornice and a new fireplace facing with bookshelves on either side. It was all done in a soft pine finish to match her antique pine furniture. Chintz curtains and a soft green rug made a very livable room. Two large small-paned windows were placed in the corner of the dining room where her plants thrived. Here she would sit in her little rocking chair and work on her rugs or whatever she was doing at the time. Just outside the dining room door, she had a patio built with bricks. Plants and flower boxes were placed around the edge. The family would gather here for many a happy occasion.

In 1949 another welcome daughter, Donna, was born to Helen and Don. Through the 1950's, Nora was able to take several trips with members of the family which she enjoyed tremendously. She had been grounded for so many years, it was like a new life opening up.

So, a peaceful decade passed into the 1960's when death began to take its toll. In 1963 Don passed away from a heart attack, and, later in the same year, a sister died. Her only son's death was a dreadful blow. It took a long time to recover. Then in succession, a brother, another sister, and finally her daughter-in-law passed away. I spent as much time as I could with her, but deep loneliness set in. Consequently, her thoughts turned to a home for the aged. She was now 87 years old. She became interested in the Presbyterian Home in Titusville some years before through a friend. It was a beautiful place, a former oil baron's home built for his bride. It had the charm that Nora loved in a home so the decision was made to become a resident. This required her selling all her personal household goods, all the antiques she had collected through the years. She gave many lovely things to members of the family, and sold the rest. I think a little bit of her heart went out the door with each cherished possession, but there was no self-pity, just determination to get it over with. And so, the rooms were empty again.

The morning of the departure for the church home, Nora and I arose early. It was a lovely fall morning, and the sun slanted across the empty rooms. My husband arrived to take us to Titusville, but before we left, she walked slowly through all the rooms upstairs and down. What memories she must have had. We waited just outside the door, and finally she came and said, "Now I am ready". Tears were very close to my eyes, but I had to match my bravery with hers and did not let them fall.

And so, the circle was closed. The door of the house in which she had started married life and in which she had spent the last twenty-three years was finally closed.

I have hit the peaks of Nora's life and rarely descended into the valleys of despair and heartache. They were there as well as valleys of happiness and contentment. She was intensely interested in all members of the family but never to the point of interference. After our mother's death, she was the matriarch. I called her the "hub of the wheel". She was a woman beyond her time but never the aggressive career type. She got things done in her own quiet way. Nora was blessed with a very active sense of humor which lightened many a family gathering. I can never pay enough tribute to her for all the kindness, understanding, and love shown to me all of her life.

Eleanora Nelson Blair died November 21st, 1977, in her 96th year and was laid to rest beside her husband who had left this world just 61 years before. I would like to think that this little lady would occupy herself rearranging things in her heavenly home, and I have a feeling the Almighty would look on with kindly indulgence.

Editor's note: The author of this story was Marjorie Marie Nelson Sanford, sister of Nora, the youngest sibling in this Nelson family. Aunt Margie, as we lovingly called her, was a gentle soul. Although she had no children of her own, she was always there for all of us who came after - daughters, sons, nieces, nephews, cousins near and far. She was our last connection to dear Nora and all of the families connected through the Nelson clan. The oldest sibling of Nora and Margie was Leah Nelson Reed who lived to be 98. Their brother, Walter Glenn Nelson, died in 1954, after making a life for himself in Long Beach, California. The sister who died in 1963 was Gertrude Nelson Brower. The other brother who passed was Joseph Sibley Nelson. The other sister who passed was Pearl Nelson Ashley. The two brothers who died young were Raymond, who died in infancy, and Roy who died at the age of nine from damaged lungs shortly after the Oil City fire and flood of 1892. Aunt Margie lived to be 96 and passed away in 1995

We descendants are lucky to be part of this heritage. It is good to know what came before us. It will help us live better lives as we move on.

www.ingramcontent.com/pod-product-compliance
Lightning Source LLC
Chambersburg PA
CBHW061250040426
42444CB00010B/2335